A Practical Guide to Critical Thinking

Essential Steps for Developing Sound Reasoning and Arguments while Overcoming Hindrances to Rational Thinking

GREG R. HASKINS

Second Edition (paperback), 2020, rev. 2.1

Second Edition (eBook), 2016

Original Edition (Skepdic.com), 2004

ISBN-13: 979-8-6496-0903-6

For inquires, email: haskins02@yahoo.com

SECOND EDITION CHANGES

The original "A Practical Guide to Critical Thinking" was hosted on Skepdic.com beginning in 2004. This second edition, available in both eBook and paperback formats, has been updated to include a new appendix on hindrances due to natural biases (Appendix 5).

CONTENTS

In Memory of Robert Todd Carroll

SPECIAL ACKNOWLEDGMENT AND PRIMARY REFERENCE SOURCES

I would like to express my deep appreciation and thanks to the late Robert Todd Carroll, PhD, for his support in making this book possible. Much of the content was based on the following references by Dr. Carroll:

- *Becoming a Critical Thinker - A Guide for the New Millennium*, 2nd Edition, Pearson Custom Publishing, 2012
- *The Skeptic's Dictionary: A Collection of Strange Beliefs, Amusing Deceptions, and Dangerous Delusions*, John Wiley & Sons, Inc., 2003.
- *The Skeptic's Dictionary* (Skepdic.com)
- *The Critical Thinker's Dictionary: Biases, Fallacies, and Illusions and What You Can Do About Them*, Lulu, 2013

Please refer to these excellent resources for a more in-depth study of critical thinking and skepticism.

Greg R. Haskins

INTRODUCTION

This book presents a concise treatise of critical thinking, embodying its most important elements into a compact, convenient, organized, and easy to understand form. It is intended as a handy go-to reference source to help anyone or any organization develop sound reasoning and arguments.

There have been many definitions of critical thinking. From a practical perspective, it can be defined as:

> **A process by which we use our knowledge and intelligence to effectively arrive at the most reasonable and justifiable positions on issues, and which endeavors to identify and overcome the numerous hindrances to rational thinking.**

Not everyone values the need for critical thinking. Often, being methodically objective is viewed as cold, sterile, and worst of all, boring. To those who say "Have faith and let your feelings guide you to the truth," or "Don't let facts get in the way of an inspiring or interesting story," these words will probably not resonate. But for those who truly understand and appreciate the importance of critical thinking, this book, including the appendices of critical thinking hindrances, can become a useful reference for daily life.

Just because you are intelligent or have great knowledge does not mean you can think critically. A profound genius may have the most irrational of beliefs or the most unreasonable of opinions. Critical thinking is about **how** we use our intelligence and knowledge to reach objective and rationale viewpoints. Opinions and beliefs based on critical thinking stand on firmer ground compared to those formulated through less rational processes. Additionally, critical thinkers are usually better equipped to make decisions and solve problems compared to those who lack this ability.

Figure 1 presents a very simplified model of the human understanding process. Basically, our *thinking processes* (No. 3) synthesize our *perceptions* (No. 2) of *reality* (No. 1) in the context of our *basic emotional needs* (No. 3A) and our *values and principles* (No. 3B) in order to reach *conclusions* (No. 4) about anything in life. Critical thinking is just one sub-process of the thinking processes (No. 3) that people may or may not employ in order to reach conclusions.

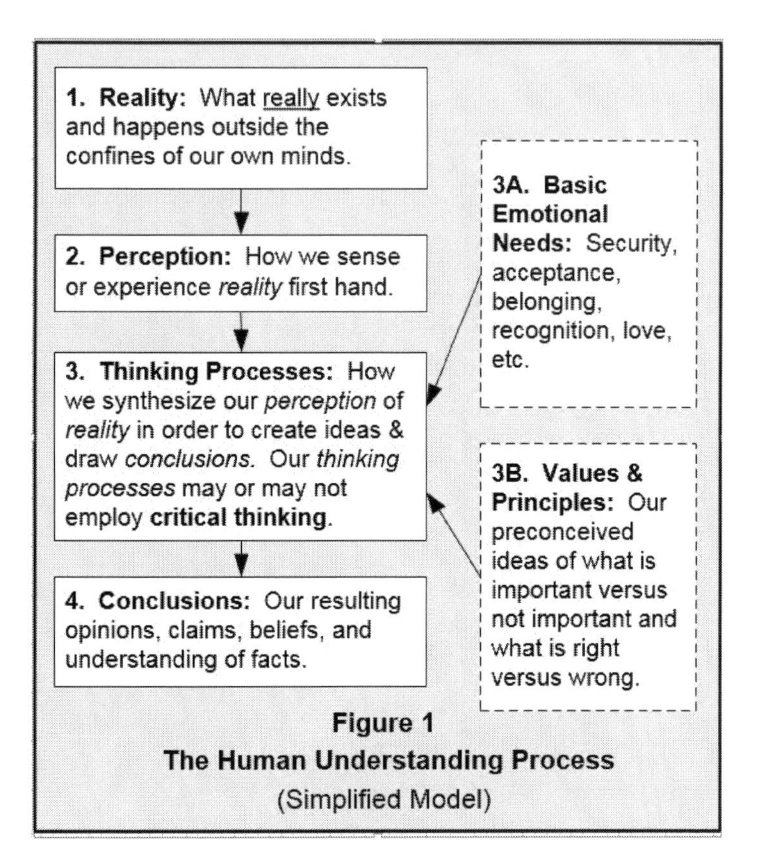

Figure 1

The Human Understanding Process

(Simplified Model)

Critical thinking is more than thinking *logically* or *analytically*; it also means thinking *rationally* or *objectively*. There is an important distinction. Logic and analysis are essentially philosophical and mathematical concepts, whereas thinking rationally and objectively are broader concepts that also embody the fields of psychology and sociology. These latter two areas address the complex effects of human behavior (e.g., hindrances) on our thinking processes.

Introduction

Becoming an accomplished critical thinker can be considered a five-step process:

1. Adopt the Attitude of a Critical Thinker
2. Recognize and Avoid Critical Thinking Hindrances
3. Identify and Characterize Arguments
4. Evaluate Information Sources
5. Evaluate Arguments

Each of these steps is described separately below.

WHAT CRITICAL THINKING IS NOT

Thinking critically is ***not*** thinking negatively with a predisposition to find fault or flaws. It is a neutral and unbiased process for evaluating claims or opinions, either someone else's or our own.

Critical thinking is ***not*** intended to make people think alike. For one reason, critical thinking is distinct from one's *values or principles* (see Figure 1), which explains why two people who are equally adept at critical thinking, but have different values or principles, can reach entirely different conclusions. Additionally, there will always be differences in *perception* and *basic emotional needs* (see Figure 1) which prevent us from all thinking the same way.

Critical thinking does ***not*** threaten one's individuality or personality. It may increase your objectivity, but it will not change who you are.

It is ***not*** a belief. Critical thinking can evaluate the validity of beliefs, but it is not a belief by itself – it is a *process*.

What Critical Thinking Is Not

Critical thinking does ***not*** discourage or replace feelings or emotional thinking. Emotions give our lives meaning, pleasure, and a sense of purpose. Critical thinking cannot possibly fulfill this role. Still, emotional decisions that are *also* critical decisions (such as deciding to get married or have children) should embody critical thinking.

Critical thinking does ***not*** blindly support everything based on science. For example, our culture is full of bogus scientific claims that are used to market everything from breakfast cereal to breast enhancement pills.

It is also important to understand that arguments based on critical thinking are ***not*** necessarily the most persuasive. Perhaps more often than not, the most persuasive arguments are those designed to appeal to our basic human/emotional needs rather than to our sense of objectivity. For that reason, it is common for highly persuasive arguments by politicians, TV evangelists, and sales people, among others, to *intentionally* lack critical thinking. (See pertinent examples in Appendices 1 through 5.)

CRITICAL THINKING STEPS

Step 1: Adopt the Attitude of a Critical Thinker

The first step to becoming a proficient critical thinker is developing the proper attitude. Such an attitude embodies the following characteristics:

- Open-mindedness
- Healthy skepticism
- Intellectual humility
- Free thinking
- High motivation

The first two characteristics may appear contradictory, but they are not. The critical thinker must be willing to investigate viewpoints different from his or her own, but at the same time recognize when to doubt claims that do not merit such investigation. A critical thinker must be neither dogmatic nor gullible. Being both *open-minded* and *skeptical* means seeking out the facts, information sources, and reasoning to support issues we intend to judge; examining issues from as many sides as possible; rationally looking for the good and bad points of the various sides examined; accepting the fact that we may be in error ourselves; and maintaining the goal of getting at the *truth* (or as close to the truth as possible), rather than trying to please others or find fault with their views. Too much skepticism will lead one to doubt everything and commit oneself to nothing, while too little will lead one to gullibility and credulousness.

Having *intellectual humility* means adhering *tentatively* to recently acquired opinions; being prepared to examine new evidence and arguments even if such examination leads one to discover flaws in one's own cherished beliefs; to stop thinking that complex issues can be reduced to matters of 'right & wrong' or 'black & white'; and to begin thinking in terms of 'degrees of certainty' or 'shades of grey'. Sometimes 'I don't know' can be the wisest position to take on an issue. As Socrates noted: *Arrogance does not befit the critical thinker.*

A critical thinker must also have an independent mind, i.e., be a *free thinker.* To think freely, one must restrain one's desire to believe because of social pressures to conform. This can be quite difficult or even impossible for some. One must be willing to ask if conformity is motivating one's belief or opinion, and if so, have the strength and courage to at least temporarily abandon one's position until he or she can complete a more objective and thorough evaluation.

Finally, a critical thinker must have a natural curiosity to further one's understanding and be *highly motivated* to put in the necessary work sufficient to evaluate the multiple sides of issues. The only way one can overcome the lack of essential knowledge on a subject is to do the necessary studying to reach a sufficient level of understanding before making judgments.

This may require the critical thinker to ask many questions, which can be an uncomfortable process for both parties. A critical thinker cannot be lazy.

Step 2: Recognize & Avoid Critical Thinking Hindrances

Each day of our lives we become exposed to things that hinder our ability to think clearly, accurately, and fairly. Some of these hindrances result from unintentional and natural human limitations, while others are clearly calculated and manipulative. Some are obvious, but most are subtle or insidious. Armed with the proper attitude (from Step 1), a critical thinker must next understand how to recognize and avoid (or mitigate) the gauntlet of deception that characterizes everyday life. These hindrances can be divided into five categories, presented in appendices at the end of this book:

- Appendix 1: Basic Human Limitations
- Appendix 2: Use of Language
- Appendix 3: Faulty Logic or Perception
- Appendix 4: Psychological and Sociological Pitfalls
- Appendix 5: Natural Biases

Each appendix provides: a) a listing of hindrances applicable to that category; b) a concise definition of each hindrance; c) illustrative examples; and d) tips to avoid or overcome such hindrances.

Basic Human Limitations (Appendix 1) applies to everyone, including the most proficient critical thinkers. These limitations remind us that we are not perfect and that our understanding of facts, perceptions, memories, built-in biases, etc., precludes us from ever seeing or understanding the world with total objectivity and clarity. The best we can do is to acquire a *sufficient* or *adequate* understanding depending on the issue at hand.

The *Use of Language* (Appendix 2) is highly relevant to critical thinking. The choice of words themselves can conceal the truth, mislead, confuse, or deceive us. From ads which guarantee easy weight loss to politicians assuring prosperity for everyone, a critical thinker must learn to recognize when words are not intended to communicate ideas or feelings, but rather to control thought and behavior.

Misconceptions due to *Faulty Logic or Perception* (Appendix 3) or *Psychological and Sociological Pitfalls* (Appendix 4) can also lead one to erroneous conclusions. A critical thinker must understand how numbers can be used to mislead; perceptions can be misinterpreted due to psychological and sociological influences; and reasoning can be twisted to gain influence and power.

Natural Biases (Appendix 5) are hindrances which we develop over time from our own unique cognitive experiences. These experiences cause us to develop our own "rules of thumb" (or heuristic) ways of learning, doing things, approaching problems and rendering judgments. Though cognitive, these natural biases are heavily influenced by our past emotional experiences.

Step 3: Identify & Characterize Arguments

At the heart of critical thinking is the ability to recognize, construct, and evaluate *arguments*. The word argument may be misleading to some. It does ***not*** mean to quarrel, complain, or disagree, even though the word is often used informally in that context. In the context of critical thinking, an argument means the presentation of a *reason(s)* to support a *conclusion*, or:

Argument = Reason + Conclusion

Argument example: Don't trust John (*conclusion*) because (*indicator*) he's a politician (*reason*).

There must be one or more reason statements and one or more conclusion statements in every argument. Depending on usage and context, reasons are synonymous with: premises, evidence, data, propositions, proofs, and verification. Again, depending on usage and context, conclusions are synonymous with: claims, actions, verdicts, propositions, and opinions.

A critical thinker must learn to pick out arguments from verbal or written communication. Sometimes arguments will have *indicators* such as 'since', 'because', 'for', 'for the reason that', and 'as indicated by' to separate the *conclusion* statement(s) from the *reason* statement(s) that follows (see above example). At other times, arguments will have *indicators* such as 'therefore', 'thus', 'so', 'hence', and 'it follows that' to separate the *reason* statement(s) from the *conclusion* statement(s) that follows. In some cases there will be no indicator words at all; the context alone will indicate if a statement is intended as a reason, a conclusion, or neither.

Formal logic divides arguments into *inductive* and *deductive* arguments. While critical thinking is an informal application of logic, the critical thinker should at least understand the fundamental differences between the two forms. If one thing *follows necessarily* from another, this implies a deductive argument. In other words, a deductive argument exists when 'B' may be logically and necessarily inferred from 'A.' For example, if one makes the statement "All bachelors are unmarried *('A')"* and "John is a bachelor *('B')*", then one can deductively reach the conclusion that John must be unmarried.

However, most arguments that one encounters in daily life are inductive. Unlike deductive arguments, inductive arguments are not 'black and white', because they do not prove their conclusions *with necessity*. Instead, they are based on *reasonable grounds* for their conclusion. A critical thinker should understand that no matter how strong the evidence in support of an inductive argument, it will never prove its conclusion by *following with necessity* or with absolute certainty. Instead, an inductive argument provides only proof to a *degree of probability or certainty*.

Arguments presented by courtroom attorneys are good examples of inductive arguments, whereupon a defendant must be found guilty *beyond a reasonable doubt* (equivalent to reasonable grounds). It is always possible that an inductive argument that has sound reasons will have an erroneous conclusion. For example, even though a jury finds a defendant guilty beyond a reasonable doubt, there is always a possibility (even if remote) that the defendant had not committed the crime. The critical thinker should assess the cogency of inductive arguments in terms of degrees of certainty instead of absolute 'right & wrong' or 'black &white'. This applies ***even if*** a 'yes/no' or 'either/or' decision must be made or judgment must be rendered on the argument.

Step 4: Evaluate Information Sources

Most arguments reference facts to support conclusions. But an argument is only as strong as its weakest link. If the facts supporting an argument are erroneous, so will be the argument. A critical thinker must have a sound approach for evaluating the validity of facts. Aside from one's personal experiences, facts are usually acquired from information sources such as eyewitness testimony or people claiming to be experts. These sources are typically cited in the media or published in reference books.

In a society where entertainment and amusement have become lifelong goals, it is often difficult to find unbiased and objective information on a subject. For example, the mass media has found "what if" journalism sells very well: *What if* the President did some horrible thing; *What if* the Secretary was motivated by some criminal behavior, etc. It is common to see reputable journalists reporting on inflammatory speculation as if it was an important news event. How can we expect to cut through the advertising, hype, spin, innuendos, speculation, distortions, and misinformation overloads on TV, radio, newspapers, magazines and the internet, in order to ascertain what is factually correct? Even some reputable publishers seem to have more interested in selling books or periodicals than confirming the truth of what they publish. So how are we to know which information sources to trust?

While there is no simple answer, a critical thinker should look for information sources which are *credible*, *unbiased*, and *accurate*. This will depend on such things as the source's *qualifications*, *integrity* and *reputation*. In order to assess these conditions, the critical thinker must seek answers to the following types of questions:

1. Does the information source have the necessary qualifications or level of understanding to make the claim (conclusion)?
2. Does the source have a reputation for accuracy?
3. Does the source have a motive for being inaccurate or overly biased?
4. Are there any reasons for questioning the honesty or integrity of the source?

If any of the answers are "no" to the first two questions or "yes" to the last two, the critical thinker should be hesitant about accepting arguments which rely on such sources for factual information. This may require additional investigation to seek out more reliable information sources.

Information sources often cite survey numbers and statistics, which are then used to support arguments. It is *extremely* easy to fool people with numbers. Since the correct application of numbers to support arguments is beyond the scope of this book, it is important that a critical thinker become educated in the fundamental principles of probability and statistics before believing statistical information supporting an argument. One does not need to be a math major to understand these principles. Some excellent books exist for the layman, such as *How to Lie With Statistics* by Darrell Huff, and *Innumeracy: Mathematical Illiteracy and Its Consequences* by John Allen Paulos. There are a few right ways and many wrong ways to sample populations, perform calculations, and report the results. If a source is biased because of self-interest in the outcome, it more often than not used one of the wrong ways. Perhaps the most important question the critical thinker should ask of any statistical result is: Were the samples taken representative of (a good cross section of) the entire target population? Also see the *Clustering Illusion* and *Law of Truly Large Numbers* in Appendix 3.

Step 5: Evaluate Arguments

The last step to critical thinking, evaluating arguments, is itself a three-step process to assess whether: 1) assumptions are warranted; 2) reasoning is relevant and sufficient, and 3) relevant information has been omitted. Each is described below.

Assumptions. Assumptions are essentially reasons implied in an argument that are taken for granted to be true. Using our earlier argument example, "Don't trust John because he's a politician", the implied assumption is that politicians cannot be trusted. The first step for evaluating arguments is to determine if there are any assumptions, and whether such assumptions are warranted or unwarranted. A *warranted assumption* is one that is either:

1. *Known* to be true; or
2. Is *reasonable* to accept without requiring another argument to support it.

An assumption is *unwarranted* if it fails to meet either of the two above criteria.

Regarding the first criterion, it may be necessary for the critical thinker to perform independent research to verify what is "known to be true." If the critical thinker, despite such research, is unable to make a determination, he or she should *not* arbitrarily assume that the assumption is unwarranted. Regarding the second criterion, a critical thinker normally evaluates the *reasonableness* of assumptions in relation to three factors: a) one's own knowledge and experience; b) the information source for the assumption; and c) the kind of claim being made.

If an argument has an unwarranted assumption, and if this assumption is *needed* to validate the argument's conclusion, the critical thinker has good cause to question the validity of the entire argument. Some of the hindrances listed in the appendices, especially Appendices 3 and 4, provide the basis for many unwarranted assumptions.

Reasoning. The second step to evaluating arguments is to assess the *relevance* and *sufficiency* of the reasoning (or evidence) in support of the argument's conclusion. It is helpful to think of "relevance" as the *quality* of the reasoning, and "sufficiency" as the *quantity* of the reasoning. Good arguments should have both quality (be relevant) and quantity (be sufficient).

It is generally easier (although not always) to pick out reasoning that is *relevant* (i.e., on the subject or logically related) than it is to determine if the reasoning is *sufficient* (i.e., enough to validate the argument). So how can one evaluate the sufficiency of reasoning (evidence) to support a conclusion? The term *reasonable doubt*, as used in a court of law, is considered a good guideline. But how does one go about determining reasonable doubt? Unfortunately, there is no easy answer, but here are some criteria. First, it is important to maintain the attitude of a critical thinker (from Step 1) and be aware of critical thinking hindrances (from Step 2). Second, ask yourself the purpose or consequences of the argument being made. This will sometimes determine how much (sufficiency) evidence is required. Third, become aware of contemporary standards of evidence for the subject. For example, you could not judge the sufficiency of evidence for a scientific claim unless you were knowledgeable of the methods and standards for testing similar scientific claims. Finally, the sufficiency of evidence should be in proportion to the strength to which the conclusion is being asserted. Thus, evidence that is <u>not</u> sufficient to support a strong conclusion (Example: John *definitely* bought the painting) may be sufficient to support a weaker conclusion (Example: John *may* have bought the painting). In these examples, if the evidence was limited to a photograph of John at an art store on the same day the painting was purchased, this evidence would not be sufficient to prove the stronger conclusion, but it may be sufficient to prove the weaker conclusion.

When evaluating multiple pieces of evidence, both pro and con, how does one *weigh* the evidence to determine if, overall, the argument is cogent? Again, there is no hard and fast rule. All else being equal, the more reliable the source (from Step 4), the more weight should be given to the evidence. Additionally, more weight should generally be given to superior evidence in terms of its relevance and sufficiency to validate the argument, all else being equal.

Many of the hindrances listed in Appendices 3 and 4 provide examples of irrelevant or insufficient reasoning.

<u>**Omissions**</u>. A cogent argument is one that is complete, in that it presents *all* relevant reasoning (evidence), not just evidence that supports the argument. Arguments that omit relevant evidence can appear to be stronger than they really are. Thus, the final step to evaluating arguments is attempting to determine if important evidence has been omitted or suppressed. Sometimes this happens unintentionally by carelessness or ignorance, but too often it is an intentional act. Since it is usually unproductive to confront arguers and ask them to disclose their omissions, the critical thinker's best course of action is usually to seek opposing arguments on the subject, which could hopefully reveal such omissions. It is a rare arguer who actively seeks out opposing views and treats them seriously, yet that is precisely what a critical thinker must do when developing his or her own arguments.

Many of the hindrances listed in Appendices 1 through 5 allow one to become easily fooled by not taking into consideration possible omissions that could invalidate an argument's conclusion.

ARGUMENT CHECKLIST

Having understood the above five-step process, a critical thinker may wish to use the following checklist when evaluating important arguments:

1. Is there any ambiguity, vagueness, or obscurity that hinders my full understanding of the argument?
2. Does the argument embody any hindrances (see Appendices 1 through 5)?
3. Is the language excessively emotional or manipulative (see language hindrances, Appendix 2)?
4. Have I separated the reasoning (evidence) and relevant assumptions/facts from background information, examples, and irrelevant information?
5. Have I determined which assumptions are warranted versus unwarranted?
6. Can I list the reasons (evidence) for the argument and any sub-arguments?
7. Have I evaluated the truth, relevance, fairness, completeness, significance, and sufficiency of the

reasons (evidence) to support the conclusion?

8. Do I need further information to make a reasonable judgment on the argument, because of omissions or other reasons?

APPENDICES OF CRITICAL THINKING HINDRANCES

APPENDIX 1

HINDRANCES DUE TO BASIC HUMAN LIMITATIONS

Confirmation Bias & Selective Thinking

Definition: The process whereby one tends to notice and look for what confirms one's beliefs, and to ignore, not look for, or undervalue the relevance of what contradicts one's beliefs.

Example: If one believes that more murders occur during a full moon, then one will tend to take notice of murders that occur during a full moon and tend *not* to take notice of murders that occur at other times.

Critical Thinking Tip: Obtain and objectively evaluate all relevant information and sides of an issue before passing judgment.

False Memories & Confabulation

Definition: Being unaware that our memories are often "manufactured" to fill in the gaps in our recollection, or that some memories of facts, over time, can be unconsciously replaced with fantasy.

Example: Police officers should *not* show a photo of a possible assailant to a witness prior to a police lineup, or the actual memory of the witness may be unconsciously replaced.

Critical Thinking Tip: Put more reliance on proven facts than memory recollection or testimonies from others. Know your own memory limitations.

Ignorance

Definition: The lack of essential background knowledge or information on a subject prior to making a judgment.

Example: One may be convinced a "yogi" has the power to levitate objects, but does not see the thin wire attached to them.

Critical Thinking Tip: Perform appropriate research on multiple sides of issues to obtain all pertinent evidence, before reaching conclusions.

Perception Limitations

Definition: Being unaware of our own perception limitations that can lead to misconceptions about reality.

Example: Looking up at the stars at night and perceiving they are as close as the moon and planets.

Critical Thinking Tip: Recognize that "seeing is not always believing" because of our sensory limitations. Know when & how to verify your observations with other sources.

Personal Biases & Prejudices

Definition: We each have personal biases and prejudices,

resulting from our own unique life experiences and worldview, which make it difficult to remain objective and think critically.

Example: Some people are biased against claims made by scientists because their worldview appears too cold and impersonal.

Critical Thinking Tip: Resist your own biases by focusing on the facts, their sources, and the reasoning in support of arguments.

Physical & Emotional Hindrances

Definition: Stress, fatigue, drugs, and related hindrances can severely affect our ability to think clearly and critically.

Example: Air traffic controllers often have difficulty making good judgments after long hours on duty

Critical Thinking Tip: Restrain from making critical decisions when extremely exhausted or stressed.

Testimonial Evidence

Definition: Relying on the testimonies and vivid anecdotes of others to substantiate one's own beliefs, even though testimonies are inherently subjective, inaccurate, unreliable, biased, and occasionally fraudulent.

Example: Dramatic stories of Bigfoot sightings do not prove the existence of Bigfoot.

Critical Thinking Tip: Resist making judgments based on testimonies alone. Extraordinary claims generally require extraordinary evidence.

APPENDIX 2

HINDRANCES DUE TO USE OF LANGUAGE

Ambiguity

Definition: A word or expression that can be understood in more than one way.

Example: From the statement "Lying expert testified at trial", is the expert a liar or is the person an expert on telling when someone is lying?

Critical Thinking Tip: If the intended meaning of an ambiguous word or expression cannot be determined, avoid making judgments.

Assuring Expressions

Definition: Using expressions that disarm you from questioning the validity of an argument.

Example: Expressions such as "As everyone knows…", and

"Common sense tells us that…"

Critical Thinking Tip: Disregard assuring expressions and instead focus on facts & reasoning that support arguments.

Doublespeak Euphemisms

Definition: The use of inoffensive words or expressions to mislead, disarm, or deceive us about unpleasant realities.

Example: Referring to a policy of mass murder as "ethnic cleansing" or the inadvertent killing of innocent people as "collateral damage."

Critical Thinking Tip: Look beyond the emotive (emotional) content and recognize the cognitive (factual) content of euphemistic words and expressions.

Doublespeak Jargon

Definition: The use of technical language to make the simple seem complex, the trivial seem profound, or the insignificant seem important, all done intentionally to impress others.

Example: Referring to a family as "a bounded plurality of role-playing individuals" or a homeless person as a "non-goal oriented member of society."

Critical Thinking Tip: Recognize the cognitive (factual) content of jargon words and expressions.

Emotive Content

Definition: Intentionally using words to arouse feelings about a subject to bias others positively or negatively, in order to gain influence or power.

Example: Naming detergents "Joy" and "Cheer" (positive), not "Dreary" and "Tedious" (negative). The military using the phrase "neutralizing the opposition" (less negative) rather than "killing" (negative).

Critical Thinking Tip: Learn to recognize and distinguish the emotive (emotional) content of language. Try to focus on reasoning and the cognitive (factual) content of language when evaluating arguments.

False Implications

Definition: Language that is clear and accurate but misleading because it suggests something false.

Example: The dairy industry cleverly expresses fat content as a percentage of weight, not of calories. Thus 2% "low" fat milk really has 31% fat when fat is measured as a percentage of calories.

Critical Thinking Tip: Understand not only the facts, but also their relevance and context.

Gobbledygook

Definition: The use of confusing non-technical language to mislead or deceive.

Example: A company using lengthy and intimidating language to simply express that if your check bounces, your receipt is voided.

Critical Thinking Tip: Recognize the cognitive (factual) content of gobbledygook words and expressions.

Hedging & Weasel Words

Definition: Language that appears to commit one to a particular view, but because of its wording, allows one to retreat from that view.

Example: President Clinton's claim that he did not have "a sexual relationship" with Monica Lewinski, in which he later explained that "engaging in sexual acts" was not "a sexual relationship."

Critical Thinking Tip: Be on the lookout for hedging language that suppresses facts supporting an argument.

Judgmental Words

Definition: Stating opinions as though they were facts, so the audience does not have to "bother" judging for themselves.

Example: The President took *justifiable* pride in signing the peace treaty.

Critical Thinking Tip: Distinguish what is *fact* from what is *opinion* in any statement or argument.

Meaningless Comparisons

Definition: Language that implies that something is superior but retreats from that view.

Example: An ad that claims a battery lasts "up to" 30% longer, but does not say it will last 30% longer, and if it did, longer than what?

Critical Thinking Tip: Avoid making judgments if it is not exactly clear what is being compared.

Vagueness

Definition: Language which is less precise than the context requires.

Example: If someone needs to be paid back tomorrow, and the borrower says "I'll pay you back *soon*", the borrower's response was too vague.

Critical Thinking Tip: Be aware of the consequences of imprecise claims based on vagueness.

APPENDIX 3

HINDRANCES DUE TO FAULTY LOGIC OR PERCEPTION

Ad Hoc Hypothesis

Definition: A hypothesis, which cannot be independently tested, is used to explain away facts that refute a theory or claim.

Example: Psi researchers often blame the "hostile thoughts" of onlookers for adversely affecting instruments measuring the alleged existence of psychic powers

Critical Thinking Tip: Put low reliance, or reserve judgment on, claims that cannot be independently tested.

Apophenia & Superstition

Definition: Erroneous perception of the connections between unrelated events.

Example: Irrationally believing that how one wears their hat while watching a football game can influence the score.

Critical Thinking Tip: Recognize the difference between *cause & effect* versus *unrelated coincidence*.

Argument from Ignorance

Definition: A logical fallacy claiming something is true because it has not been proven false.

Example: Believing that there must be life on Mars because no one has proved that there is not life on Mars.

Critical Thinking Tip: Do not believe a proposition simply because it cannot be proven false.

Begging the Question

Definition: A fallacious form of arguing in which one assumes to be true something that one is trying to prove.

Example: A man claiming that paranormal phenomena exist because he has had experiences that he can only explain as paranormal.

Critical Thinking Tip: Recognize when an argument assumes to be true something it is attempting to prove. When this occurs, seek alternative explanations.

Clustering Illusion & Texas Sharpshooter Fallacy

Definition: The erroneous impression that random events that occur in clusters are not random.

Example: In ESP experiments, a "water witcher" using dowsing may find water at a slightly higher-than-chance rate over a brief period of time, and mistakenly assume this proves dowsing really works.

Critical Thinking Tip: Understand the basic principles of probability & statistics. Recognize when numbers are being used correctly & objectively versus incorrectly & with bias.

False Analogies

Definition: Making illogical analogies to support the validity of a particular claim.

Example: Arguing that two children sharing the same bedroom is wrong because double-celling of criminals in a penitentiary can lead to bad behavior.

Critical Thinking Tip: Learn to recognize the faulty assumptions behind false analogies.

Forer Effect

Definition: The tendency to accept vague personality descriptions that can be applicable to most people as uniquely applicable to oneself.

Example: Astrology readings, intended for people of a specific sign, can be applicable to most individuals. This effect usually works in conjunction with 'Self-Deception' and 'Wishful Thinking.'

Critical Thinking Tip: Critically evaluate if personality characterizations are truly unique to you, or could apply to most people.

Gambler's Fallacy

Definition: The fallacy that something with fixed probabilities will increase or decrease depending upon recent occurrences.

Example: The misconception that picking lottery numbers that have not yet been picked will increase your chances of winning.

Critical Thinking Tip: Learn to recognize and distinguish events that have *fixed* versus *variable* probabilities.

Irrelevant Comparisons

Definition: Making a comparison that is irrelevant or inappropriate.

Example: Making a claim that Printer A makes better copies than Printer B, while ignoring the important fact that only Printer B can also fax, copy, and scan.

Critical Thinking Tip: Be sure to compare "apples with apples."

Law of Truly Large Numbers

Definition: A failure to understand that with a large enough sample, many seemingly unlikely coincidences are in fact *likely* coincidences, i.e., likely to happen.

Example: The alleged uniqueness of the number 11 to the September 11 can be mathematically shown to be not unusual at all, and merely a game to play with people's minds.

Critical Thinking Tip: Understand the basic principles of probability & statistics. Recognize when numbers are being used correctly & objectively versus incorrectly & with bias to support an argument.

Non Sequitur

Definition: Reasons given to support a claim that are irrelevant.

Example: To say "I am afraid of water, so I will take up flying."

Critical Thinking Tip: Lean to recognize when arguments are supported by irrelevant reasons.

Pareidolia

Definition: A type of misperception involving a vague stimulus being perceived as something clear, distinct, and highly significant.

Example: Most UFO, Bigfoot, and Elvis sightings.

Critical Thinking Tip: Recognize that a vague perception of a strange event can have many possible explanations. Seek alternative explanations that are *more likely* rather than more emotionally appealing.

Post Hoc Fallacy

Definition: The mistaken notion that because one thing happened after another, the first event caused the second event.

Example: Believing that beating drums during a solar eclipse will cause the sun to return to the sky.

Critical Thinking Tip: Try to identify the known or possible causal mechanisms of observed effects, starting with those that are more likely.

Pragmatic Fallacy

Definition: Arguing something is true because "it works," even though the causality between this something and the outcome are not demonstrated.

Example: After using a magnetic belt for a while, a woman notices her back pain is less, even though there may be a dozen other reasons for the reduced back pain.

Critical Thinking Tip: Try to identify known or possible causal mechanisms for observed effects, starting with those that are *more likely*, not more emotionally appealing.

Regressive Fallacy

Definition: Failing to take into account the natural and inevitable fluctuations of things when assessing cause and effect.

Example: Assuming a man's neck pain consistently fluctuates over time, he will most likely try new remedies when the pain is at its worst point, then perhaps incorrectly assume that the pain got better because of the new remedy.

Critical Thinking Tip: Try to identify and understand recurring behavioral patterns before making judgments about recently observed events.

Slippery Slope Fallacy

Definition: An argument that *assumes* an adverse chain of events will occur, but offers no proof.

Example: "Because regulators have controlled smoking in public places, their ultimate goal is to control everything else in our lives."

Critical Thinking Tip: Evaluate the logic supporting an alleged adverse chain of events.

APPENDIX 4

HINDRANCES DUE TO PSYCHOLOGICAL AND SOCIOLOGICAL PITFALLS

Ad Hominem Fallacy

Definition: Criticizing the *person* making an argument, not the argument itself.

Example: "You should not believe a word my opponent says because he is just bitter because I am ahead in the polls."

Critical Thinking Tip: Focus on reasons & facts that support an argument, *not* the person making the argument. Independently verify supporting facts if the source is in question.

Ad Populum, Bandwagon Fallacy

Definition: An appeal to the *popularity* of the claim as a reason for accepting the claim.

Example: Thousands of years ago the average person believed that the world was flat simply because most other people believed so.

Critical Thinking Tip: A valid claim should be based on sound arguments, not popularity.

Communal Reinforcement

Definition: The process by which a claim, independent of its validity, becomes a strong belief through repeated assertion by members of a community.

Example: The communally reinforced yet mistaken belief that one can get rid of cancer simply by visualization and humor alone.

Critical Thinking Tip: Do not follow the crowd simply because if gives you a feeling of acceptance and emotional security. Think for yourself.

Emotional Appeals

Definition: Making *irrelevant* emotional appeals to accept a claim, since emotion often influences people more effectively than logical reasoning.

Example: Advertisements that appeal to one's vanity, pity, guilt, fear, or desire for pleasure, while providing no logical reasons why their product is superior to competitors' products.

Critical Thinking Tip: If an argument requires a logical reason to support its claim, do not accept emotional appeals as sufficient evidence to support it.

Evading the Issue, Red Herring

Definition: If one has been accused of wrongdoing, diverting attention to an issue *irrelevant* to the one at hand.

Example: The President making jokes about his own character in order to disarm his critics & evade having to defend his foreign policy.

Critical Thinking Tip: Learn to recognize evasion, which implies a direct attempt to avoid facing an issue.

Fallacy of False Dilemma, Either/Or Fallacy

Definition: Intentionally restricting the number of alternatives, thereby omitting relevant alternatives from consideration.

Example: "You are either with us, or with the terrorists!"

Critical Thinking Tip: Seek opposing arguments on the subject which may reveal the existence of other viable alternatives.

Irrelevant Appeal to Authority

Definition: An attempt to get a controversial claim accepted on the basis of it being supported by an admirable or respectable person.

Example: "Since the Pope thinks capital punishment is morally justified, it must be morally justified."

Critical Thinking Tip: Recognize that any appeal to authority is irrelevant to providing logical grounds and facts to support an argument.

Lawsuit Censorship

Definition: Repressing free speech and critical thinking by instilling fear through the threat of lawsuits.

Example: Journalist Andrew Skolnick was sued for his investigative reporting of Maharishi Mahesh Yogi and his Transcendental Meditation Movement.

Critical Thinking Tip: If a counter-argument is not readily available, don't assume it does not exist. It could be suppressed by special interests.

Moses Syndrome, Suggestibility, Conformity, & Deferring Judgment

Definition: Promises of happiness, security, power, wealth, health, beauty, etc., made again and again in a confident manner, by charismatic people with prestige, tend to be believed uncritically and without argument or proof.

Example: Hitler convinced an entire country to follow his dream of making Germany great, which included the subjugation and massacring of Jews. Also, Jim Jones of the *Peoples Temple* doomsday cult convinced 914 of its members to commit suicide.

Critical Thinking Tip: Resist the human tendency to believe a charismatic leader simply because he/she appeals to your basic human needs. Seek alternate views & reliable sources for facts and objective reasoning to support arguments.

Poisoning the Well

Definition: Creating a prejudicial atmosphere against the opposition, making it difficult for the opponent to be received fairly.

Example: "Anyone who supports removing troops from Iraq is a traitor!"

Critical Thinking Tip: When evaluating an argument, focus on the argument, not prejudicial remarks.

Political Censorship

Definition: Repressing free speech, distorting facts, or "cherry picking" facts to support a biased political viewpoint or dogmatic belief.

Example: When politicians intentionally present selectively chosen facts or distorted facts on a particular issue, then conclusions reached by the public may be biased or faulty.

Critical Thinking Tip: Learn all sides of an issue. People can present deceptively logical arguments that are built upon the selective choosing of facts.

Positive Outcome Bias

Definition: The tendency for researchers and journalists to publish research with positive outcomes between two or more variables, while not publishing research that shows no effects at all.

Example: The media will publish the results of single study showing a nutritional supplement can reduce anxiety, but it will not publish the results of five other studies showing the same supplement has no effect on reducing anxiety.

Critical Thinking Tip: Put more reliance on claims which use methods that seek to eliminate positive outcome bias. Seek information from sources that do not have a biased interest in the results.

Shoehorning

Definition: The process of force-fitting some current event, after the fact, into one's personal, political, or religious agenda.

Example: Jerry Falwell and Pat Robertson claimed that American civil liberties groups, feminists, homosexuals and abortionists bear partial responsibility for September 11 because their immoral behavior has turned God's anger toward America.

Critical Thinking Tip: Understand the motives or agenda of people or organizations prior to making judgments on their arguments.

Sunk-Cost Fallacy

Definition: The psychological phenomenon of continuing to hold on to a hopeless investment for fear that what has been invested so far will be lost.

Example: Lyndon Johnson continued to commit many thousands of U.S. soldiers to Vietnam even after he was convinced the U.S. could never defeat the Viet Cong.

Critical Thinking Tip: Do not allow your fear and disgrace of taking a loss cause you to take even a bigger loss.

Wishful Thinking & Self Deception

Definition: The process of misinterpreting facts, reports, events, perceptions, etc. because we want them to be true (or not true).

Example: 94% of university professors think they are better at their jobs than their colleagues.

Critical Thinking Tip: Understand that our individual view of what we think is true can be strongly biased by our needs, fears, ego, worldview, etc.

APPENDIX 5

HINDRANCES DUE TO NATURAL BIASES

Affect Bias (Affect Heuristic)

Definition: Gut feeling or rule of thumb (heuristic) decisions which are influenced by past emotional experiences or ideas.

Example: Paying more for airline travel insurance that covers death from just terrorist acts versus all possible causes because "terrorist acts" has strong negative emotive content.

Critical Thinking Tip: Recognize your own emotional biases before making a decision or rendering a judgment.

Anchoring effect

Definition: Gut feeling or rule of thumb (heuristic) decisions which are influenced by comparisons to a preconceived "anchor point."

Example: Buying a coat because the original price on the label has been greatly reduced, giving one the impression of getting a bargain, all because the original high price was accepted as an anchor.

Critical Thinking Tip: Recognize when judgments or decisions are based on comparisons to an anchor point. If so, critically evaluate if that anchor point is a valid basis for comparison.

Availability Error

Definition: Gut feeling or rule of thumb (heuristic) decisions based on the first idea that comes to mind (snap judgments).

Example: After being exposed to frightening news stories of jihadist terrorism, immediately suspecting a Middle Eastern person you see on the street as a terrorist.

Critical Thinking Tip: Generally do not go with the first idea that comes to mind. Consider other alternatives while recognizing your own emotional biases.

Backfire Effect

Definition: When confronted with evidence that conflicts with one's beliefs, one holds the original beliefs even more strongly.

Example: After watching news stories which reveal flaws in your cherished presidential candidate, you support your candidate even more.

Critical Thinking Tip: Evaluate the validity of information sources and arguments (Steps 4 and 5) before rendering a judgment. Remain flexible to changing your judgment if warranted based on sound information and arguments.

Continued Influence Effect

Definition: This is an extension of the Backfire Effect in which one finds out later that evidence conflicting with one's belief is actually sound or true, yet one still clings to the original belief.

Example: Weeks after watching negative ads demonizing one's cherished presidential candidate, one learns the facts were correct after all, yet it does not influence one's support for that candidate.

Critical Thinking Tip: Seek out credible, unbiased, and accurate information (Step 4) to obtain facts to support valid arguments (Step 5) to support (or change) one's beliefs or opinions.

Hindsight Bias

Definition: The tendency to construct one's memory after the fact (or interpret the meaning of something said in the past) according to currently known facts and one's current beliefs.

Example: After the Challenger space shuttle disaster that killed seven astronauts in 1986, hindsight bias was used by followers of Nostradamus to claim that his writings had predicted this disaster.

Critical Thinking Tip: Put more reliance on proven facts than memory recollection or testimonies from others. Recognize that any appeal to authority does not provide logical grounds and facts to support an argument.

Inattentional Blindness (Inattention Blindness)

Definition: An inability to perceive something that is within one's direct perceptual field because one is focused on something else.

Example: Counting how many times a basketball is passed from one team member to another, while being oblivious to someone walking through the scene wearing a gorilla suit.

Critical Thinking Tip: Remain aware of other factors affecting the current situation despite being focused on a specific activity or goal.

Motivated Reasoning

Definition: An extension of Confirmation Bias (Appendix 1) where one not only confirms what he/she believes while ignoring contrary information, but also develops elaborate rationalizations to justify their belief.

Example: Believing the Apollo moon landings were a hoax by focusing attention on extravagant conspiracy theories while ignoring sound scientific evidence.

Critical Thinking Tip: Obtain and objectively evaluate all relevant information and sides of an issue before passing judgment.

Nasty Effect

Definition: The process by which negative, uncivil and hurtful dialog has intuitive appeal to some, making it easier to accept points of view without doing any significant study or research.

Example: Radio talk shows making repeatedly vile comments against anyone or any position that does not support their political viewpoints.

Critical Thinking Tip: Seek out credible, unbiased, and accurate information sources (Step 4) to obtain facts to support valid arguments (Step 5) to justify (or change) one's opinions.

Proportionality Bias

Definition: A tendency to believe that causes are proportional to effects in magnitude, e.g. extreme events with momentous consequences have extreme, momentous causes, while mundane events have mundane causes.

Example: Believing it is inconceivable that a mundane person like Lee Harvey Oswald could have acted alone in performing the momentous act of assassinating President Kennedy, rationalizing a massive conspiracy must be involved, despite the lack of hard evidence.

Critical Thinking Tip: Accept that extreme events sometimes have mundane causes, and vice versa. Be wary of conspiracy theories, especially those which are not based on hard facts and sound reasoning.

Recency Bias

Definition: The tendency to think that trends and patterns we observe in the recent past will continue in the future, particularly the long term future.

Example: Believing the stock market will continue to do well for years because it has been doing well for the past three months.

Critical Thinking Tip: Recognize there are often complex dynamic factors beyond our direct knowledge, understanding or measurement which greatly limit our ability to predict the future, especially the long term future.

Representativeness Bias

Definition: Gut feeling or rule of thumb (heuristic) judgment of ideas through comparison to one's standard way of thinking or a representative idea, then deciding their merits based on how well they match up with this model. Related to Anchoring Effect.

Example: Believing that a quiet, shy, reserved, and self-effacing, man is more likely a brain surgeon than a salesman, because one's stereotype of a salesman is of an outgoing, gregarious person. But the odds of *any* given man being a salesman are much higher than the odds of being a brain surgeon.

Critical Thinking Tip: Understand the limitations of making biased stereotype decisions based on gut feelings or adherence to a standard way of thinking. Seek out credible, unbiased, and accurate information (Step 4) before rendering an opinion.

Selection Bias

Definition: Selection of individuals, groups or data for analysis in such a way that proper randomization is not achieved, thereby ensuring that the sample obtained is not representative of the population intended to be analyzed.

Example: Talk show hosts who poll callers on their position on political issues generally obtain biased results because such shows attract a portion of the population that is not representative of the country as a whole.

Critical Thinking Tip: Before accepting the results of studies, activities or polls which involve outside participants, evaluate the extent to which participants are representative of the population intended to be analyzed versus a biased subset.

Single Cause Bias/ Fallacy/ Illusion

Definition: When understanding complex phenomena, the tendency to accept: a single cause explanation (*bias*); a single cause based on no evidence (*fallacy*); or a single cause based on testimonials, biased scientific evidence, or communal reinforcement (*illusion*).

Example: The tendency to think that complex phenomena or situations such as alcoholism, cancer, mental illness, airplane accidents, economic recessions, political scandals, etc. are each due to a distinct single cause.

Critical Thinking Tip: Recognize that complex phenomena and situations almost always result from multiple causal factors. Understand the limitations of testimonials, biased scientific evidence, or communal reinforcement for a single cause explanation.

Made in the USA
Middletown, DE
09 January 2023